Behind the Sun

Sukhdev Kaur Dhade

PublishAmerica
Baltimore

ISBN: 1-4241-7068-0
PUBLISHED BY PUBLISHAMERICA, LLLP
www.publishamerica.com
Baltimore

Printed in the United States of America

To
My
Family
And
My
Parents

Cordially
Love to
My son
Dr. Amanbir Dhade
Who encourages
Poetry

Contents

Same

God color same
I dream, I see the dream
Every day same and same

Christine different, Muslim different
Sikh different, Hindu different
Religion different, culture different
Blood color is same
I dream, I see the dream
Every day same and same
God color is same

Living different, fashion different
Lyrics different, music different
Rhythm of sound is same
I dream, I see the dream
Every day same and same
God color is same

Black different, white different
Tall different, small different
Heart color is same
I dream, I see the dream
Every day same and same
God color is same

Sea different, rivers different
Country different, towns different
Water colour is same
I dream, I see the dream
Every day same and same

Different people, different worlds
God color is same
I dream, I see the dream
Every day same and same
God color is same

New Year Night

On New Year eve
Looking at the sky
Touching the stars, making a wish
A wish of peace, for this world
I find a song to write
For the New Year night

On New Year eve
I find myself crying
My pen picks up the tears
Flows in the words of laugh
Listening to the laughter sounds
On New Year night
I love a song to write

On New Year eve
I find myself mad
My pen picks up the anger and
Flows in the words of love
In the love of love
On New Year night
I love a song to write

On New Year eve
I find myself sad
My pen picks up my sorrows
Flows in the words of happiness

Through my pen
On New Year night
I find a song to write

On New Year eve
I find myself hurt
My pen picks up the wounds
Flows in the words of heals
With the ink of love
On New Year night
I love a song to write

Like to Sing

I like to sing to the world
East to west, north to south
I like to sing, at the beginning of the year
I like to sing till end of the year

Days has gone, days will come
Months has gone, months will come
I like to sing from beginning to the end

I like to sing for black and white
I like to sing for day and night
I like to sing when white snow is on the ground
I like to sing when green grass on the ground

I like to sing to my life
I like to sing to my death
On the way to the heaven
Reaching the star
Beyond the sky
I like to sing till I die
I like to sing live or die
I like to sing for you forever and ever

I like to sing at beginning of the day
I like to sing at the end of the day
I like to sing when you are away
I like to sing till you come
I like to sing when you love
I like to sing for you forever and ever

Who Is?

Once upon a time
I was sad
I felt a soft touch
Over my ears
Touched my cheeks
Wiped my tears
I tried to see the touch
Wondered who is?

Once upon a time
I was angry
I heard a soft tone
Under my chin
Opened my lips
Echoed a laugh
I tried to hear the laugh
Wondered who is?

Once upon a time
I was lost
I felt a soft walk
Behind my shadow
Touched my feet
Turned my way
I tried to find the way
Wondered who is?

I opened my eyes
Dream of tomorrow
To heal my heart
A ray in the dark
Blowing wind
Flying to the moon
Near the stars
Moonlight tears
Cloudy laugh
Golden chains on my feet
Turned to butterflies of my heart
Plucking the sorrows
With the thorns of roses
Behind the milky stars
Wondered who is?

Life's Turn

Courage of life's turns in
One's life is life
A smile swallows
The rivers of sorrows

My Poem

My poem is
Translation of feeling
In one's words
Writing of soul
In a language of heart
Writing pen
Filled with ink
Of love
For the one's
Who lost the courage?
In Life

Limitless

Free nature
Free thoughts are limitless
Free love in the heart is limitless
Free air is limitless
Free water is limitless
Free earth is limitless
Free sun is limitless
Free moon is limitless
Free view is limitless
Free thoughts are limitless

Away from that limitless freedom
I am caged on 20th floor office building
Looking through a tiny window
For the limitless freedom
Starving to dive
In the limitless free ocean
For a ride
To fly
In the sky

Only a Breath

Tiny part of my father
Grew in the tomb
Of my mother
For nine months
Entered in this world
With a cry
Knowing no love
No laugh
Only a breath

To My Love

Pain of heart
Blended in the feeling
In the ink of my pen
Flowing through the words
Touching the breeze
Holding the wings
Of stormy wind
Fly to the sky
Beyond the stars
To my love

I walk to the middle of night
Wait in garden in the moonlight
Looking at the moon
Through the mountains
Holing the clouds
A massage in broken star
In empty lap
A milky star trying to reach me
Pulling hand from my pocket
With a speechless voice

With no witness
Holding a pearl
See that diminish of dark
Behind the tree
Veil of moonlight wrapped

The trees of flowers
My love of rose
In the bush of heart

Time

I see the clock
Needles of time
Approaching the mid night

Needles of my clock
Blending the feeling
In empty lap

Needles show the night time
My broken lovely time
I listen my breaking heart
Like a glass
Sounds can

Black Storm

Black stormy night
Lightning, thunder
Ears listen the
Pulse of my heart
When lightning flash
On the wall
I see the needles of my clock
Small needle
When lightning strike
To break the wall

Literature of Life

No chance to read poetry
No school to learn poems
Life journey witnessed
The happenings
Unseen love story
Affection sorrow seen
Sound of walk
Feeless touch
Heart middle

Speechless Words

Your speechless words
Echoed in my ears
Your sleepless nights
Slept in my nights
Your sightless eyes
Eyed in my eyes
My loveless heart
Blended in my heart

Behind the Sun

Behind the stars
Under the ocean
Reaching to the lava
Digging the earth
With mirror walls
Opened the door of my heart

I see
A face in the mirror
Deep eyes
Roses behind the thorns
Spreading the fragrance
With the fans of the winds

Above the clouds
Walking through the rainbow
Colors in my soul
A child in the lap
Of moonlight
Catching the shadows of unknown
Fitting the pieces in the sky
Behind the sun
To get a sip of love
On the earth

Dew Drops Tears

That stormy night
Wind was blowing
Trees were falling
Speechless words echoed
I love you

That stormy night
Moon was glowing
Stars were falling
Speechless lips shouted
I love you

That stormy night
Rain was falling
Light was flashing
Silent clouds thunder
I love you

That stormy night
Looking around
Sleepless night
Echoed
I love you

Storm flew
Blue sky, Moonlight stars
Dew drops tears
Morning touch
I love you

Love of Affection

Empty lap of my heart
Pure love of affection
Soul meeting
Live in the heart
Touch less relation

Inner blood of feeling
Beneath the ocean
Sleepless thought
Lava flash
Blend sun in moon

Moonlight in a ray
Empty lap of
My heart
Cries to say
My love of affection
For you and you

Behind the Beauty

For security of beauty
I was bowing
Suddenly stopped

You are beautiful,
Not a God

Desire for affection
Love of life
Thank to my eyes
Who blessed you attraction

Pay wishes to my heart but no cheats
Who let you live in my beats

Your stars of love were dim
Some may ask my feel
Losing boat of love in sin

Winning steps, loss of game
Lonely meetings sad and same

True love is never sorrow
Happy delight bond of tomorrow

Beauty is in the dove
No replacement of love

You are beautiful
Not a God

Let Go

Let go
New love of your night
Let go my love
Prisoner of feeling
Let go my thought
Morning sun blends

In my love
New hope of night
Sleep of freedom
Freshness of sight
Eyes stare to see

My face
Face of love
Wrapped in
Your heart

Found on the Street

I was in school
I was playing
And number one
When I made a goal
Behind my back, someone shouted
Don't play with the bastard
He was found on the street

Beautiful girl fell in love
Offered her hand
In the church, priest asked
Any body have objection
Behind my back, someone yelled
Do not marry to the bastard
He was found on the street

Beautiful baby born
Looking at the angel face
I turned to give a kiss
Voice drummed into my ear
Do not let him kiss
He was found on the street

Who was my bastard father
Shouted under the water
He was angel with the wings
He was moon in the sky
He was mine

Dark cloud roared in the sky
He was a god's son
That's why
He was found on the street

Hope

High, large building
Burning flame of desire
Under the blanket
Dark night
Pedestrian walking
On the street

Little far away
In the corner
Under the blanket
Ravish dream
A hoping hope
In the half closed tearless eyes
Holding the hopeless hope
Looking at the lights of city
Through a hole of blanket
A dying hope
Dreaming the dreamless hope

Once he was a hope
Nothing seems to work
In difficult times
Mars and Saturn
Made room in his house
Like indebted hooligan
Son of light
Moon of night

No fight
No sight
Today is just a hope
In the corner of the street
Under the blanket
Home of a homeless hope

Fibbing

Standing for a moment
Enjoying the stillness of the night
Far away in the sky
Imaginary talks to herself
Among the stars, behind the sun
Facing in veil of moonlight

A love of companion
Climbing to hold the wind
Catching the fan of kite
In that shiny stormy night
Burst to grab a sip of light
In that dark bright night

Looking through the window
With crumbling feeling
Walling her shared secrets
Holding head with tight fist
Kissing the antiques of
Timid feelings of her soul

With unwavering gaze in
High fly clouds gilt frame
Singing a song in a voice
To reach for a nest
In the moon
A love to enjoy in light of candlelight

Pearly Heart

Single horn honking
Reached in my ear
It must be a girl
Next door in the red car

In front of my door
I see the shadow
Long hair
I opened the door
It must be the girl
Next door in the red car

I reached my pocket
A number was written
On a piece of paper
Dial the number
It must be my dream
Girl in the red car

I looked behind, there
A girl standing
I reach her lips, a sweet kiss
It must be a kiss of my dream
A kiss of a girl
In the red car

In her shadow
In the water
Looking down in the sea
A glimpse of mermaid
Mirror of glazing eyes
Saying to me
I am your dream
Girl in the red car

Ice Over the River

In the glazing of morning sun
Wintry cold wind
Making river water run
No, no, fish cried
Let's hide under the water

No, no crocodile laughed
Crazy fish
Who can hide under the water
Breathing swimming in the water
Sleeping with open eyes
I can hide under the water

No, no crocodile shouted

God tells me I can breath
God tells me I can sleep
God tells me I can creep
Fish madam
I can't hide under the water

God wants me breath in water
God wants me sleep in water
God wants me to creep in water
I can hide under the water
My shelter my water

Casino

Both needles on the clock
See as one at mid night
Over the tower
Middle of city
In the casino
Dance of red green light

Full drinks glass with
Empty hearts
Glazing through the light

Across the hall
Unknown faces
Wondering eyes
Searching the flame
Just a sight
Only tonight
May be some one

A love of life
Future bright
Just in the casino
A touch of sight
Just to night

Poetry

Poetry is creation
Emotion of heart
Feelings compile
In soul of file
Flows in the blood of veins
Heats the body
Body of creation

Poetry is a feeling
Poem of love
Injustice of innocents
Cruelty of crime
Within the soul
Digging deep inside
For someone to write
Song of creation

Poetry is a lava
Burning glory
Middle of heart
Pain of a little story

With a touch
Of someone
To cool the wounds
With ice of love
Heart is soft
Limited lava

Poetry is daffodil
Butterflies
Taste inside
The colorful flower
Red, yellow and white
All there
None for a heartless
None makes you see

Favor

Storm blowing
Do me favor
Do not go
Someone may stop

You are the one
Who said that
Love is world
Love is life
Today my loss
My game of heart
It is your loss too

Sun of desert burn the feet
Cool the wounds of the cheat
Love is not a game
Troubling soul will be same
Storm blowing
Someone may stop him go
Love is meeting of true minds
Morning nights
Morning sights
Wandering whirls lost the finds

Beauty

She did not walk
Suddenly she was walking
Over the clouds
With the wind

With wings of birds
Bathing in the sun that sets before her eyes
Drinking the sorrows of sudden joys
Her fluttering desire

Bandaging the memory pain
Speechless train of thought
Fire and sword
Weaker in her beauty caught

Swift touch walks
Over the clouds
She mirrored in the moon
And smirked
Nature gave her the beauty
To smile away the sorrows
And wounding pain of tomorrows

Dreaming Life

His eyes were neither open nor closed
Were not moving from the spot
In the night of stars
Sleeping on moonlight spread
In the thoughts of memories
Not being scared from sorrow

Together we will
Reduce some sorrows
Life blossom into flowers
Love everybody and make all yours
In the swing of open air
Sun was gone long ago

Birds returned to their nests
Accompany night shadow
Of her gone
Desire flame to meet
Never want to know
Whether he was awake or sleep.

Just Me

Want to be bird, so she fly
Want to be sun, so she shine
Want to be lion, so she fight
Want to be snake, so she bite

Afraid from height
Scared from nights
Too gentle to fight
Too noble to bite

Rubbing her eyes
She woke up screaming
Just me is fine
Being me is fine

Meeting Forever

Meet anyone
Anybody
Anywhere

God gave power to meet
Anyone, anybody, anywhere

Friends leave, see them in soul
Perhaps to see them in our dreams

No one can stop, steel or borrow
Your dreams
They are yours
Only yours
What other snatch from you
You get them back
In your dreams
Blind love is possession
Almighty obstacles
Lord is creator
Lord is preserver
Humble one bows in front
Predictable, they are doomed

New Page

Come and play their role
In the corner, in the city
Parent stage
Children play
Run the show

Love of life in the age
Every morning is new page
Read stars
Everyday of burning case
Searching forever
Peace, love and justice
Plunge the feeling in your heart
Sharply and deeply
To sing a song in lovely place

God

God gave a sight
Just see through the eyes
Was found on the street
A beautiful nobody
Gave me wish
She has to leave with my open eyes
I saw my wish in her tear

I was same
I wanted to sleep
For the show
Whistling air
Icing sun
With a glow
Global walk
In the light
Water the grow
I might be slow
But God gave me the power to dream

Unknown Forest

All walk through in
From one side to other
Parents hold hand to lead
In youth, company of my friends
Accompanying seed

Holding hand in the age
Cross the unknown forest
This is a life
In the forest where
Loins, snakes, animals live
Became part of journey
Be friends
Crossing unknown forest
Wish to Live

Oceans Exceed

In the heart of need
Love under the soul
Oceans exceed

Expect to grow
Like to hide
Under the leaves of show

Pains of mercy story
Blooming flower with the glow
Drinking the pain of the glory

Losing love was a curse
Saying good-bye was the worse
You are the cause of hold
Shy and shaky feelings of bold

In the heart of need
Love under the soul
Oceans exceed

A Thought of Right

In dark night
Snowflakes
Under the sky
Near the star
Shadow of kite

Red rose face
Thirsty lips
Sparkling eyes
Feel of night

Under the coat
Soft touch
Gentle touch
Feel of might

Way to sky
Feel of deep
Dark spot
In the moon
Wish to bright

In the wind
Stormy light
See the thorn
In the rose
Wondering thought
Thought of right

See You

Moon shatter into glass
Glass of mirror
I see you in the mirror
Mirroring the stars
I see you in my sky

Flower growing in the garden
Full of butterflies
I see you near the flower
Enjoying the fragrance of petals
I see you in the try

Birds chirping in the morning
Sweet songs
I love you in my sonnets
Singing the song
I see you in a fly

Walking near the ocean
Full of tides
I see you catching the wave
Backing tears of eyes in the water
I see you in the cry

Counting the petals
Humming my sonnets
Wrapping the wind in the tide
Over silver moonlight
I see you shinning in the sky

Betrayed Love

Dance prickly dance
A needle in the heart
Dance to love
Sing a song
Song for love

Deep deep try
No tears to cry
Sleep in mystic
Like a cuckoo
Wait for rain to fall

Wounded wings to fly
High in the sky
Search the love
Love of life
Dance prickly dance
To live in the lies
Of the betrayed love
Dane prickly dance

A Man of My Thought

In the morning
New year day
Boiling water in the kettle
For some one some body

Snowflakes on the window
Ignite the sun in the heart
Burn the tears in the ice
Cool the water in the fire

Sound of lava
Melted glacier
With a touch
Of the unspoken word

Feel in the wind
Listen the thunder
Talking with the eyes
Seeing through the voice

Feel the beat of my heart
Miles away
Dreaming my mind
Some one
A man of my thought

Burning Feet

Place near the river
Walking in the rain
Muddy road, sinking feet
Deep down in the earth
Volcano touch
I cried what's there
Under my burning feet

Dark night in the jungle
Wind blowing
Hear scary sounds
Fire under the tree
I smell the smoke
I shouted what's there
Under my burning feet

Moonlight in the dark
Breeze misted around
My face
Touching ground
Iced the wounds
Of my burning feet

Must Be the Cat

Picking the morning paper
In my front door
I see the cat crossing my way

Morning walk in the forest
In the grass, I see a rabbit
Peaceful sleeping
In the nest, I see a bird
Bird breathing
Under the shrub, I see a snake
Snake creeping
Running back, scared to death
I think of my luck
It must be the cat crossing my way

Sitting in the chair
Reading the paper, I see a car
Driving car
In the Hall, I see the bar
Drinking in the bar, I see my car
Over the bridge, I see a fall
Running back, scared to talk
I think of my luck
It must be the cat crossing my way

Leaning the head
Closing my eyes, I see a house
House of my dream
In the garden, I see a flower
Blooming color
In the flower, I see a butterfly
Enjoying the taste
Taste of my love
Running back, scared to see
I think of my luck
It must be the cat crossing my way

Rainbow

Shiny sand of desert
A deer
Running for a water sip
Mirage run fast
Just little more
Reach the water
Quench the thirst

I am not that mirage to run
See the rain
Feel the pain

I will
Search the rainbow in the sky
Over the cloud
After the rain
Meeting the earth with the sea

Color of thought
Green walk to the land
With white cool the sand
Whistle blue in the sea
Open the heart with a key
Strength of my orange key

Leaving all the colors for
The heartless
Painless
Loveless
To color their toes
Wake the dream of coming rainbow

Waiting Forever

In the sun across the road
Over the mountains, across the field
Under the bridge
Pale face, wide eyes

Scattered hair, over a shadow
Ice the water in the fire
Shadow light in the sun
Mute fool cry in love
Walk among the long grass
And singing
Yes—in the dream
I had a voice
Low and sad
Waiting for you
Under the bridge
Pearly tears
Countless bad
Pieced in courage

Smile Promise

Lets swear
Keep on smiling
Passion in your veins
Climb the mountain
From the light of death
Should not be scared
Your beauty shine
Like pearl in the shell
The days of happiness come
The nights of sorrows gone
Reality of dream
See the moon in her heart
Stars in the eyes
She hoped for a dream
A dream of love

Scudding Clouds

She opened the back door
Cold invaded her heart
She felt like tourist
Trapped in a Cave
Trying to escape
She walked from room to room
Feeling homeless
Opulent to excite
Looking through the window
See the shadow of green trees
Walling the beautiful
Red, yellow and white roses

In the sky
Scudding clouds creating
Illusion of a racing moon

Beneath her shy and mockery smile
A light heart thought crossed her mind
Discerned a core of genuine love
Just walling racing moon
With scudding clouds

Thirst

In the sunny night
I had a line to write

There was a moony ghost
Like to shine with a boast

Jungle was a burning verse
Sitting crying in hearse

Rainbow was drawing a line
Webbing poems of mine

I was writing little knowing
Dark clouds water the growing
I was filling my inner wanting
Stars were ready for the granting

I was counting my matter
Curing pain and wounds of flatter

Dreams of dark morrow
Washing tears of my sorrow

Blowing wind cry to take
Frame the wall of happy make

Color of night was black
Ink of light was a lack

Desire

A love must go away
Wait to come
Hope to get
In the eyes of heart
A ray to live for me
Again and again
When I love
A desire, deep down in the soul
Must go away
For tomorrow to see
Again and again
Desire to live
In the jungle of memory
Refusing the crumbling walls
Lurking shadow of sorrow
Swallow in my blood
No one with me any more
Combed and stored the sorrows
In a desire to live

Wound speak
In the throne of memory
My pulse is dipping
I pick from my past
Deserted place
Death was ashamed
A desire, deep down in the soul

Must go away
For tomorrow to see
Again and again
Desire to live

Wing Ride

My heart wanted to fly
Away with her into the night
Holding edge of silky feather

In the sky, full of star
Riding on the wings
Kissing the lips tightly
Leaned towards each other

Looking into the blue twinkling eyes
Pounding on the door of the my heart
Taking deep breath
I loved her deeply
Every lovely wish of her
I whispered in her ear
I was sharply sleeping in her arms
I felt two hot tears
Squeezed down my cheeks and flicked
I heard her say "Sorry" I did not mean this happen.

Gone

Groaning in the night
Beautiful with
Solidity of her voice
Mute cry in her tone
She is free of that in dream
And will be mine forever

Flying for the sight
Smiling with proud
Song of her choice
Cheerful try was ever gone
She is sweet in my dream
Forbidden to love me forever and ever

Her gone made me mad
Inside my heart
Vision of her touch
Witness of her twinkling eyes
She was walking on the light
Alone again and lonely for ever

Connecting Doors

Walking down the street
In the shadow of doubt
Beautiful memories of my heart
Gone away without
Connecting doors

Beautiful thought was there
A love of life
With shadow of fear
Countless beats of my heart
Gone away without
Connecting doors

In the nest of my heart
A feel of empty
Filled with love
Fly away with wind
Gone away without
Connecting doors

Nodding head reaching over
Stared at her in the moonlight
I asked courageously
Where are my years of love
His privy whispered
Gone away without
Connecting doors

Time Slip

I was drinking with eyes
Not let time slip
Keeping eyes open
Moon may eclipse

I came back from her door
With flash of my mind
My love may touch
Blossoming of kind

Heart had met
In the Boat of love cyclone
Free meet of feeling
Shy, sharp and alone

Delicate buds
Ready to depart
In the burning rain
Desire to love in my heart

Moonshine in the stars
Life is shaken
Wounds may heel
Pain not taken

Innocent

She was dying in a shame
Spots of guilt of his name

Mind was filled with woe
Breaking heart so and so

He can curse with a skill
A smile was enough to kill

He was living in a pleasure
Enjoying beauty of her treasure

No one can cheat or betray
Cover the falls of his translate

He was calling himself a chief
He knew to smile in grief

He claimed her very dearly
Keeping her happy and nearly

He did not win anyone before
Never learned to stop for more

Someone winning was his loss
Ocean was his aim to cross

She was ready for everything to give
Truth and love was enough to live

Others happiness was her doom
Dream to think there may be a room

Playing life was not a sport
Her wish was her living resort

Feelings of life was no esteem
Innocent love was her deem

LaVergne, TN USA
24 January 2010
170995LV00004B/39/A